WHERE AM I?

Bible Places in Rhyme

WHERE AM I?

Bible Places in Rhyme

By

MABEL H. NANCE

AUTHOR OF

*Go Till You Miss, Who Am I? Easy-to-Play Bible Games,
Guess My Name, Kid's Bible Quiz, Bible Quizzes for
Preschoolers, Brain-Teasers for Teen-Agers*

MOODY PRESS

CHICAGO

ISBN: 0-8024-9435-8

1973 Printing

Printed in the United States of America

1

When Paul preached in this city,
Some of his hearers believed;
He dwelt in his own hired house,
All that came to him he received.

*Answer*_____

2

Peter, Andrew, and Philip
Were from this city in Galilee;
Here Jesus touched a blind man,
His second touch caused him to see.

*Answer*_____

3

To this mountain Moses went.
From Pisgah God did show
The land God promised Abraham;
Thither Moses could not go.

*Answer*_____

4

There was great joy in this city,
Many people to Christ, Philip won;
Simon the sorcerer also believed,
Beheld miracles and signs which were done.

*Answer*_____

5

It was here one day by this river,
That Jabin's army was led;
Sisera got down off his chariot,
And to Jael's tent he fled.

*Answer*_____

6

It was here the man sick of palsy
Through the roof was borne by four;
Jesus saw their faith and healed him
Whom they couldn't get through the door.

*Answer*_____

7

The five kings feared greatly
This city in battle array;
At the word of Joshua,
The sun stood still for a day.

*Answer*_____

8

Here in this mount Saul's army
Before the Philistines fled;
Saul took his sword, fell on it,
When he saw that his sons were dead.

*Answer*_____

9

The people started to murmur,
When the waters were bitter here;
Then Moses sweetened the waters,
To prove that the Lord was near.

*Answer*_____

When the people moved from Marah,
They came unto this place then;
And found twelve fountains of water,
And palm trees threescore and ten.

*Answer*_____

One day Saul disguised himself,
Consulted a witch in this place;
She raised Samuel from the dead,
Saul to the ground bowed his face.

*Answer*_____

They found a man named Simon,
From this city in Libya was he;
He was compelled to carry
Jesus' cross to Calvary.

*Answer*_____

Cornelius had a vision,
Talked to an angel of the Lord;
Here Peter preached to Gentiles.
On them God's Spirit was poured.

*Answer*_____

14

Paul preached here in this city,
Many to the Lord were turned;
The sorcerers brought their books,
Before all men they were burned.

*Answer*_____

15

In this city in Cilicia,
A man was born named Saul;
The law Gamaliel taught him,
God changed his name to Paul.

*Answer*_____

"My punishment is greater
Than I can bear," Cain said;
From the presence of the Lord,
To this land he fled.

*Answer*_____

Cain built the first city,
And when the building was done
He called the name of the city
After the name of his son.

*Answer*_____

Abraham was a stranger.
At the time of Sarah's death
He bought this cave for burial
From the sons of Heth.

*Answer*_____

It was here in this city
The boy Jesus was raised;
At his spiritual wisdom
His parents were amazed.

*Answer*_____

To this city of Macedonia,
Paul and Silas did go;
The Jews searched daily the Scriptures
Whether those things were so.

*Answer*_____

From this mount Jesus ascended
In a cloud, out of their sight;
While they stood gazing toward heaven,
Two men stood by in apparel white.

*Answer*_____

22

Here in the city of David,
Joseph and Mary came;
Our Saviour was born in a manger,
The angel gave Jesus His name.

*Answer*_____

23

The angel of the Lord told Philip
To go to this desert place;
After hearing the Scripture expounded,
The eunuch rejoiced in God's grace.

*Answer*_____

24

Waters prevailed upon the earth
That God in Heaven created;
Upon this mount the ark did rest,
When the waters were abated.

*Answer*_____

A certain man told Joseph
Where his brothers had gone one day;
Finally Joseph found them here,
Feeding their flocks by the way.

*Answer*_____

26

Hidden and buried in a tent,
Were silver and the wedge of gold;
Achan confessed, and all that he had
Was buried in this valley, we're told.

*Answer*_____

27

The Lord said unto Joshua,
"Fear not, neither be thou dismayed."
With strategy, this city was taken
By an ambush of men unafraid.

*Answer*_____

Dorcas was a seamstress,
Till death had closed her eyes;
Kneeling by her, Peter prayed,
And said to her, "Arise."

*Answer*_____

Jesus looking from the cross,
Saw John at His mother's side;
The beloved disciple cared for her
After Christ was crucified.

*Answer*_____

"Stand upright on thy feet,"
Paul to the cripple said;
Later on, Paul was stoned,
Drawn out of this city for dead.

*Answer*_____

"To the unknown God," Paul saw,
Inscribed on an altar here;
The truth of Christ's resurrection,
He told without trembling or fear.

*Answer*_____

The people were not allowed to come
On this mount where God spoke the law;
All of the people stood afar off,
When the smoking mountain they saw.

*Answer*_____

Sarah saw Hagar's son Ishmael
Mocking young Isaac one day;
This thing was grievous to Abraham,
To this wilderness he sent them away.

*Answer*_____

In this place, Jacob took stones
To use for his pillows that night;
He dreamed of a ladder to Heaven,
And woke in the morning with fright.

*Answer*_____

Jacob's name was changed to Israel,
After wrestling in this place;
Striving here for spiritual power,
He had seen God face to face.

*Answer*_____

The Apostles Paul and Barnabas,
Worshiped with this church a year;
Many people these men taught,
The disciples called Christians first here.

*Answer*_____

37

The risen Lord revealed Himself
To His disciples by this sea;
They fished all night, caught nothing,
Then, a hundred and fifty-three.

*Answer*_____

38

Upon this isle the Apostle John
Saw the holy city foursquare;
No need of candle, Christ is the light,
No death, nor crying there.

*Answer*_____

39

In a cave in this wilderness,
David did Saul no hurt;
David could have killed Saul,
He only cut off his skirt.

*Answer*_____

"Get thee out of thy country,"
God told Abram, son of Terah;
Nephew Lot departed too,
With Abram and his wife Sarai.

*Answer*_____

To this mountain Isaac went,
With his father Abraham;
He started to offer his only son,
When God provided a ram.

*Answer*_____

Seven years of famine began,
According as Joseph had said;
All other lands had famine,
In this land there was bread.

*Answer*_____

"Wherefore smitest thou thy fellow?"
Moses to a Hebrew man said;
Moses feared when his sin was known,
From Egypt to this land he fled.

*Answer*_____

44

An earthquake shook the prison,
After Paul and Silas prayed;
The jailer would have killed himself,
For he was sore afraid.

*Answer*_____

45

Paul preached here till midnight,
The disciples had broken bread;
Eutychus fell from the third loft,
Paul raised him from the dead.

*Answer*_____

46

Here Jesus said to Peter,
"Let down your nets for a draught";
When they launched out in the deep,
Their nets broke with fishes caught.

*Answer*_____

47

Jesus met this blind man,
Anointed his eyes with clay;
To this pool He sent him,
He was healed on the Sabbath day.

*Answer*_____

48

The nobleman asked Jesus
To come and heal his son;
His fever left that very hour,
This household Jesus won.

*Answer*_____

"This land flows with milk and honey,"
Caleb and Joshua said;
The ten other spies were frightened,
Brought an evil report instead.

*Answer*_____

God planted a beautiful garden,
In it he formed a man;
A woman he made for a helpmeet,
Marriage was part of God's plan.

*Answer*_____

The Lord came to see the tower
Being built in the city here;
He then confounded their language,
And scattered them far and near.

*Answer*_____

52

Lot was told by two angels,
To escape ere this city burned;
His wife looked back from behind him,
To a pillar of salt she turned.

*Answer*_____

53

In the contest at this mount,
God in Heaven did not fail;
Elijah determined the true God,
And killed the prophets of Baal.

*Answer*_____

54

When Moses was upon this mount,
The burning bush he saw;
While tending flocks of Jethro,
Who was his father-in-law.

*Answer*_____

55

Along the road to this village,
Two men with Jesus walked;
They knew not then the risen Lord
Was the One with Whom they talked.

*Answer*_____

56

The word of the Lord came to Jonah,
From God's presence he started to flee;
In this city he finally preached,
After being cast forth in the sea.

*Answer*_____

57

A man named Job lived in this land,
Upright, God-fearing was he;
God allowed Satan to take all he had,
This testing Job bore patiently.

*Answer*_____

When Paul came here from Athens,
Then there were tentmakers three;
For Aquila and Priscilla
Had the same craft as he.

*Answer*_____

In this garden Jesus knelt,
The three disciples were there;
They failed to watch, were sleeping,
Each time He rose from prayer.

*Answer*_____

A light shone down from Heaven,
Saul heard, "Why persecutest thou me?"
Led by men to this city,
For three days he could not see.

*Answer*_____

61

The cripple lying by this pool,
With Jesus had a talk;
On the Sabbath, Jesus said,
"Take up thy bed and walk."

*Answer*_____

62

Zacchaeus was a wealthy man,
Little of stature was he;
He learned that Jesus was coming,
And climbed a sycamore tree.

*Answer*_____

63

In this country, Elimelech died,
Naomi's two sons then did marry;
Later, they died, so Naomi and Ruth
In this place no longer would tarry.

*Answer*_____

64

Here king Ahasuerus reigned ,
In a place with court so grand;
He was wroth when the queen refused
To come at his royal command.

*Answer*_____

65

Shadrach, Meshach, Abed-nego,
In the fiery furnace were cast;
God's mighty deliverance was seen
As they came from the burning blast.

*Answer*_____

66

Naaman was a mighty man,
Though stubborn, he did yield;
In this river seven times he dipped,
From leprosy he was healed.

*Answer*_____

67

When God's chosen people,
From the land of Egypt did flee;
They crossed safely on dry land,
The Egyptians drowned in this sea.

*Answer*_____

68

Here Jesus called to Lazarus,
Who had been four days in the cave;
His sisters, Mary and Martha,
Saw him rise again from the grave.

*Answer*_____

69

The disciples and Jesus' mother,
At the marriage feast did dine;
Here Jesus performed his first miracle,
When He turned the water to wine.

*Answer*_____

When eight days were accomplished,
According to God's holy Word;
Baby Jesus was brought by His parents,
To present Him before the Lord.

*Answer*_____

Here lived a secret disciple,
Who wrapped Jesus in linen clothes;
And placed Him in his new tomb,
Perfumed with myrrh and aloes.

*Answer*_____

A certain woman named Lydia,
A seller of purple was she;
When Paul preached here in Asia,
She accepted the Lord readily.

*Answer*_____

ANSWERS

1. Rome (Acts 28:16, 30-31)
2. Bethsaida (John 1:44; Mark 8:22-25)
3. Nebo (Deut. 34:1, 4-5)
4. Samaria (Acts 8:5-6, 9-13)
5. Kishon (Judges 4:7, 15)
6. Capernaum (Mark 2:3-5)
7. Gibeon (Joshua 10:2, 12)
8. Mount Gilboa (I Sam. 31:1-4)
9. Marah (Exodus 15:23-25)
10. Elim (Exodus 15:27)
11. Endor (I Sam. 28:7-20)
12. Cyrene (Matt. 27:32)
13. Caesarea (Acts 10:1, 3, 44)
14. Ephesus (Acts 19:1, 19)
15. Tarsus (Acts 22:3)
16. Nod (Gen. 4:13, 16)
17. Enoch (Gen. 4:17)
18. Machpelah (Gen. 23:4-11)
19. Nazareth (Luke 2:40, 48)
20. Berea (Acts 17:11, 13)
21. Olives, or Olivet (Acts 1:9-10)
22. Bethlehem (Luke 2:4-7)
23. Gaza (Acts 8:25-28)
24. Ararat (Gen. 8:1-4)
25. Dothan (Gen. 37:17)
26. Achor (Joshua 7:26)
27. Ai (Joshua 8:1)
28. Joppa (Acts 9:37, 40)
29. Golgotha, or Calvary (John 19:27)

30. Lystra (Acts 14:10)
31. Athens, on Mars' hill (Acts 17:23)
32. Sinai (Exodus 19:12, 17-18)
33. Beer-sheba (Gen. 21:9-10, 14)
34. Bethel (Gen. 28:11-12, 19)
35. Penuel (Gen. 32:24)
36. Antioch (Acts 11:26)
37. Tiberias or Galilee (John 21:3-11)
38. Patmos (Rev. 1)
39. En-gedi (I Sam. 24:1, 4)
40. Ur of the Chaldees (Gen. 11:31)
41. Moriah (Gen. 22:9, 13)
42. Egypt (Gen. 41:30)
43. Midian (Exodus 2:13, 15)
44. Philippi (Acts 16:26)
45. Troas (Acts 20:6, 9)
46. Lake Gennesaret (Luke 5:1, 6)
47. Pool of Siloam (John 9:7)
48. Capernaum (John 4:49)
49. Canaan (Num. 13:2, 27)
50. Eden (Gen. 2:8-22)
51. Babel (Gen. 11:8-9)
52. Sodom (Gen. 19:26)
53. Carmel (I Kings 18:38-40)
54. Horeb (Exodus 3:2)
55. Emmaus (Luke 24:13-16)
56. Nineveh (Jonah 1:2-3)
57. Uz (Job 1:15-22)
58. Corinth (Acts 18:1-2)
59. Gethsemane (Matt. 26:36, 40)
60. Damascus (Acts 9:3-4)

61. Bethesda at Jerusalem (John 5:8-9)
62. Jericho (Luke 19:5)
63. Moab (Ruth 1:6)
64. Shushan (Esther 1:2-12)
65. Babylon (Dan. 3:20)
66. Jordan (II Kings 5:10, 14)
67. Red Sea (Exodus 14:22, 27)
68. Bethany (John 11:44)
69. Cana of Galilee (John 2:2, 8-9)
70. Jerusalem Temple (Luke 2:21-22)
71. Arimathaea (John 19:38-39)
72. Thyatira (Acts 16:14)